HEROES
YOUR COMMUNITY AWAITS
AF479599
DARREN COUNCIL

Heroes: Your Community Awaits

Table of Contents

Synopsis

This book is all about me - encouraging you to be the best version of yourself possible. Do you ever see a vision of what you're made of but need the right people in your ear to help you get there? You may need help seeing something and feel stuck with no purpose. This book is for you too! Do you need help finding people to motivate and encourage you? This interactive workbook will show you how to find your heroes, including the Hero within. Take a seat, grab something to write with - and prepare to shake up the world. This workbook is suitable for young men between the ages of 15-25.

"Sometimes they come to us, many times we have to search for them, but most of the time the hero is in us."

- Darren Council

Dedication

I want to dedicate this book to my son, Darren Jr. I named you after me because our name means great. I love you, son. I also want to dedicate it to all of the young black men who don't have the presence of a strong male role model in their life right now. I wrote this for you. To my Mom and Grandma, thank you for always being there. Last but not least, I want to give a Huge shout-out to my daughters and my Boo for being my biggest cheerleaders.

Ready, Set, Go! When I first married, I desired to be around different types of insightful people. However, I didn't know how to meet them. I instantly asked myself where these folks were. Why didn't I have them in my life?

What if I had the type of people that I know now back then? Maybe I would have made better decisions as a teen, and perhaps my business wouldn't have failed. Maybe when I came back from Iraq, I would have gotten mental health help, along with everything the military would have offered me for being a disabled veteran. I sit and think from time to time...How my life would be so different now.

We always wonder What if? But people say that everything happens for a reason. Having the right advisors in your corner can set you up for a level of success that money can't buy. Yes, your story is important.

Your story and the perseverance it took you to get through will be the strength someone else will need to live another day.

Have you ever been in a place where you felt that if you had the wisdom to make the right moves, the dream that you always envisioned would become a reality? I've been there. I've been there more than a couple of times. You want to reach out to someone who would help you make a decision, but you currently need that person in your corner.

And because of disappointment, you may think that true heroes don't exist. Let me put your mind at ease. I felt the same way. When I was a teen, in my eyes, heroes were scarce, and no male figure was in my corner rooting for me. I just had to figure out how to be a man on my own, and guess what? I did! And I am still figuring it out. But the difference is... I've learned how to locate my heroes.

And you know what else? I have learned how to become MY HERO too.

Get your pen ready because this book is about to change your life. I'm giving you something that no one ever gave me, and that's a head start. Ready, Set, Go!

Chapter 1

What is a Hero?

Hero, *defined by dictionary.com: is a person who, in the opinion of others, has special achievements, abilities, or personal qualities and is regarded as a role model or ideal:*

Story Time:

A good friend of mine reminds me of when I was his Hero in one of the most vulnerable times in his life. He had just lost his 21-year-old son in a car accident. He shares this story with me enough to remind me that checking up on your friends during tough times is essential. People assumed he needed time to cope when he needed people to check on him. He allowed himself to go into deep holes he couldn't always bring himself out of.

When you get so low, and to a point where you feel like you can't make it, a hero could be vital in picking you up and getting you back into gear. I am so grateful that God used me as a hero for someone who needed it the most.

Like in the movies, heroes save people from the villain (your negative version of yourself), but they also help individuals in their secret, private distress.

Everyone needs a supporter in their corner. Having a Hero encourages you through the tough times, and in this book, I will help you figure out how to find your heroes, including the one in you.

Your Turn

As you were reading Chapter 1, Name one person that popped into your head as a hero. How has that person been a hero to you?

____

____

____

____

Tell about a time when you were in a low place. Who helped you out of it?

____

____

____

____

Do you consider yourself a hero? Tell me about a time when you were a hero to someone.

____

____

____

____

Chapter 2

Why I needed a Hero

I remember seeing it. The exact place where I wanted to be. I was so excited to be there. I was standing in front of a crowd as a "Subject Matter Expert," talking about the journey that I had to go through. I wasn't standing there in front of this large crowd because I wanted to be a celebrity. I was standing there to talk about my marriage and how having a fun, lasting relationship is possible.

Then I woke up and realized I wasn't in front of anyone. It was all a dream. I realized I didn't have the wisdom or resources I needed to get to that stage. That's why I needed one.

Here is what I figured out, I didn't have to be on this journey alone. There is no possible way I could do it on my own. The truth is...Someone can help you through, and someone will. Finding people around you who try to do things alone is easy. Most times, it could work out better. They get burned out fast, and stress levels are heightened much quicker than someone who may have a team. It's easier to tackle a problem or hurdle with the right people in your corner. However, frustration can be confirmed when you're going through this alone, and if not dealt with, it could lead to depression.

Let me Help You, Help You...

GET ON A TEAM! FIND YOUR SQUAD!

❖ These are the people who want to see you prosper.

Do you want to know why I needed a hero? Because I realized that I could not accomplish my purpose on my own.

Everyone has a purpose and a God-given gift inside of them. Your gift is more potent than you could ever imagine. It can only torment you if you don't implement things to make it happen. God never put you on this earth for you to handle your purpose alone. You have everything you need to accomplish the things that you are destined to do. The question is, **have you opened your eyes to see what's right in front of you?** Do you even know what your gift is?

I needed someone to help me navigate through the thoughts in my mind during this season of the unknown. I imagined a time when I was succeeding. My version of success is simple: Touring the world and encouraging folks to be better versions of themselves for themselves and those under their influence. So immediately after my vision (which was often happening), I realized I didn't have the resources to get there. When you're in this mindset, you have to encourage yourself. You have to remember the end goal. That will keep you focused on your goals and the things you need to be "The Hero."

Story Time:

Donnell Johns is the first G1 National Guard Sergeant Major. He owns a business called Avision Worldwide and is devoted to supporting veterans. He has become a great friend and someone that has encouraged me.

I saw Donnell at a County building finishing up a board meeting. I met him at a business mixer a few months prior, and he was doing great things. I saw him doing Facebook lives, and I wanted to do them as well. I would do Facebook live posts, but I needed to be more consistent with it. I would get discouraged because I would always get people texting or calling me telling me that: the light on my video wasn't bright enough, I needed a haircut, the video was too long, etc...

Side Note:

Do you ever have people telling you...that what your trying isn't good enough? What you may have thought was great courage to start, others are telling you it isn't good enough. And the craziest part is, they aren't even doing anything themselves. Block out the noise.

Back to my story: When I saw Donell at the County building, I knew I had to ask him how he gets the courage and consistency to do videos all the time. Donnell and I have similar backgrounds (both served in the Army National Guard), so it was easy for us to connect. We had a similar language. I started to tell him what I wanted to do, and through that, he gave me some direct feedback. He said you have a problem with "finishing," and I can help you with that. Although I didn't want to hear about my weaknesses at the time, I was most grateful that he offered his coaching and expertise.

Sometimes the truth hurts. But if you can get past those limited beliefs and see the end goal, you will be much closer to your dream.

Let me Help You, Help You...

- ❖ If you have a dream you can complete alone, you're not dreaming big enough.

Your Turn

Why do you think finding a mentor/coach is essential?

____

____

____

____

Now visualize yourself in the place where you have always wanted to be. Describe what that looks like.

____

____

____

____

Call the oldest person in your family, and ask them how they made it.

____

____

____

____

How will you continue the legacy or change the narrative of your family line?

____

____

____

____

Chapter 3

What do They look like

When I was about 12-13, I remember my mother sending my brother and me to stay the weekend with one of her best friends/coworkers, Mr. Anthony (real name withheld). He would take us fishing, to the park to play ball, teach us how to wash a car (elbow grease was misunderstood concept), and plenty of other things. Just an overall positive Black male figure. But he probably will never know or even remember the one thing he taught me that stays with me. One day, Mr. A, his lady, my brother, and I were on our way to the park. There was an apparent conflict between the adults, but our kid's brains couldn't fully see the real issue. But for the 32-minute car ride to the park, Mr. A played Nelly Feat. Kelly Rowland - Dilemma over and over and over again. And sang every word every time. So much to the point that his empty outstretched hand was eventually filled with hers, and the conflict was gone as fast as it came...or so we thought, lol.

Mr. A was a hero in my eyes.....He taught me the power of being humble. All great men and leaders must remain humble and admit fault while asking for forgiveness.

Khari Johnson (KJ)

Sometimes we need to figure out what they look like.

Refrain from discounting someone that may not fit the mold of what you think a hero is supposed to look like. Can you think of an example where someone got it mixed up? And please note, having lots of money or a fancy car doesn't make a person a hero. Appearances often rule our perception of what we believe a hero is supposed to look like.

Heroes come from different ethnicities, economic brackets, backgrounds, and ages. My current heroes are just that. One of my best friends is 3 years younger than me, and we met in high school. Montis (Munch) Lash greeted my family and me with open arms. When we first met, I remember his desire to be great. Now he is a high school football coach giving back and mentoring young men to aspire to be great. On top of all that, he is wearing a humongous ring because his team won their state championship.

What to look for?

Find someone that models your perception of what greatness looks like. **How do I do that? What do your friends currently do? How can you model some of the good things they are doing and use that in your life? Follow someone on social media who is doing what you are good at and see what makes them different. If they have a book, buy it. What are things that they do that can motivate you to do better?**

Let me Help You, Help You…

❖ You gotta learn from Greatness to be Great!

Think about it...

Think about what you want to be. What makes you happy? What would you do even if dollars were not attached? Once you begin doing those things, people will start to gravitate toward you and give you the encouragement you didn't see coming. Sometimes you must be in the right place and surround yourself with the right people.

Story Time:

I am currently going through a time where I'm acknowledging my mental health. This past year has been a roller coaster of emotions for me. I have been expressing to friends and family how I'm feeling in an attempt to get through. During one visit with one of my friends, I started talking about this and felt like they saw my soul. They saw everything I was going through, and she spoke about it. I was so emotional that I couldn't contain myself. Something hits differently when someone talks directly about your circumstance. You feel confirmation, and you feel like hope is possible.

Your Turn

What would you do if money wasn't involved?

How honest are you with yourself regarding your flaws?

How are your friends encouraging you in your thoughts and ideas?
Are they encouraging you to be better?

While reading this Chapter, did another hero come to mind?

____

____

____

____

Chapter 4

How my "Aha" moments changed my life

Have you ever gotten that light bulb moment? Better yet, that Aha moment when you realize that you have what it takes? Sometimes you must understand yourself before the "Real You" can step forward.

How my life turned out

When Lawanda and I first married, I had no idea what I wanted to be. However, she had her whole life planned out, and I couldn't figure out how she seemed to have it all together. However, I decided that while I was figuring it out, I would support Lawanda in everything she did. That has been the key to our marriage. Once I started to share with my wife what I wanted to be, I realized that there was a better version of me that I wanted to explore. It's ok to support others and engage in their dreams. You may find your talent while serving others. As I started to actively engage in Lawanda's dreams and aspirations, I had to get involved in a way that I felt comfortable and a way that I would be most effective. Once I started to do this, I began to have serious fun greeting people and engaging with them. I realized that I was most effective at handling the back end of the business. Knowing that, I increased my focus and started to hone in on those things. That's when it seemed easy to get A's in college. Life becomes easier when you can focus on what you are called to do. You can save time. Someone's life may depend on it.

Your Turn

Sit down in a quiet place, and focus on your strengths. List three strengths. If you don't know, ask a close friend or family member.

1.

____

____

____

____

2.

____

____

____

____

3.

____

____

____

____

Let me Help You, Help You…

- ❖ One decision can change your whole life! STAY Focused!

How my life could have turned out….

Have you ever been in a life-altering position? So life-altering that your future could be forever changed once the decision is made? That's what happened to me. I remember when I was around 15 years old. I was trying to fit in. I wanted friends. This afternoon wasn't any different.

It was a typical day, and I was approached by a good friend of mine along with a friend that I knew was always in trouble. I can't remember the exact words, but the short conversation went something like this:

My friends: "Hey Darren, you want to go to the store with us?"

That sentence was harmless, but it was something about how they said it that didn't sit well with me, and I couldn't figure out why. That was until one of them showed me the gun that they had. I told them I wouldn't go and would catch them when they returned. Yup, you can call me a punk if you want. I was a punk that day, and I'm glad I was because…. they didn't come straight back. They had committed armed robbery and got caught. **That decision could have changed my life.**

Your Turn

What's a recent decision you've made that was or could have been life-altering?

Why are you in my Life?

Look at the people in your circle, and glean what you need from the relationship. Everyone that is now in your life - is in it for a reason. Some may be in it for a long time, and others may be in it for a season (nobody knows how long a person will be in their life). I have learned to nurture every relationship I am in to "maximize" its value. Every relationship has value. Every one of my friends, I have determined why they are in my life. I also recognize why I am in other people's lives and ensure that I add value to theirs. Most times, this isn't a conversation that I have with them - but this is something that I noticed by spending time with them. This has allowed me to know how and when to ask friends for things. This has nothing to do with physical money but everything to do with mental funds. This isn't about using one another. It's about propelling one another for greatness. **If you have friends, figure out ways to empower them and make healthy deposits into their lives. On the flip side, if they are not making healthy deposits in your life...it's time you find someone who can.**

Your Turn

Make a list of your closest friends. Write down ways you can make healthy deposits into their life.

Chapter 5

Are you ready to be a Hero?

Who is currently looking at you to be their Hero?

What do you need to do to get them back on their journey or encourage them to stay on it? Recognize who looks at you to be a hero in their life. It may be a younger sibling, younger cousin, a friend in the neighborhood, etc. Remember, someone is always watching you. Someone will always look at you to determine how you're making it.

Story Time:

My journey started when I finally decided to make a change for myself. I was 19 years old. I had moved out of my mom's house, living in income-based housing, and working at Mcdonalds, making $6.50 an hour. I was driving a 1969 Plymouth Valiant. However, even with all this, or some may say that lack thereof, I had the compassion and desire to take in my younger cousin.

I had the opportunity to make a difference in someone's life. Recognizing what you DO have versus what you don't have will make a difference. If I had focused on what I didn't have, I would have never brought my cousin to live with me. Do you recognize that you do things you didn't even know that you had the wisdom or the example to do? I needed to gain the expertise to take my cousin in. However, I loved him enough, so I decided to try it. Under the circumstances, I wish I could have provided for him, but I needed the long-term goals and the finances to take care of him.

I told myself that I had to do better with my life. Working at Mcdonald's is not where I wanted to be for the rest of my life.

That's when I decided to get into the military. Through the military, I received the confidence that I desired. It was about something other than money. I showed the men in my family that living the life you want is possible.

Your Turn

What practical advice can you pass down that will help the next generation from making the same mistake you made? What would you tell the younger version of you to watch out for?

____

____

____

____

How can you be a leader amongst your peers?

____

____

____

____

What can you do right now to begin leading within your family?

____

____

____

____

The change will happen in your life. How will you explain this to your family?

____

____

____

____

What legacy do you want to leave?

____

____

____

____

Chapter 6

I'm a Black Male suffering in plain sight.

Unfortunately, suffering in plain sight is the systematic norm for many people of color. Looking back on my 10 years serving this country as a United States Marine, I suffered in plain sight my entire enlistment. Prejudices overrule the feelings and oppression that minorities deal with as service members. Throughout my military career, I witnessed individuals speak up about racism. In return, they were scrutinized and threatened with punishment and or mistreatment. The reality of having color was ever-present, and the injustices that went along were heartbreaking and disappointing. No longer will I ever keep quiet when it comes to racism. Hopefully, suppose we all continue to speak up and stand firm against racism. In that case, minorities will begin to feel welcome and equal so that all of our service members can serve without the depressing thought of unfair treatment.

Kadeem Walker - Marine Vet

This book is dedicated to all young black males suffering in plain sight.

2020 was a traumatizing year for most Black Americans, including myself. I must be careful about what I say here because some stories and memories can trigger emotions. It's tough when you have to go around daily with the afterthought that I may be perceived at any given moment as a threat because of my skin color. Simple things like jogging in my neighborhood, reaching for my wallet, or asking questions. "Can you please tell me why you pulled me over, officer?"

When I meet new people in an unfamiliar setting, In a joking but profound way, I tell them, you do understand that I am black, right? When we were house hunting, I always prefaced with...How many of "US" live in this neighborhood?

I am saying all this because there are too many hashtags. None of us can stand to watch another viral video of a black man getting killed or mistreated. But I want you to know that as an Adult, we share the same feelings, hurt, and anger every time something happens, just as you do. It is our norm. But the question is, how will you respond to it all? Even with this, you can't bottle it up until it explodes. You have to take action.

Can you find a way to be a hero, even in this? The quick answer is; Yes, you can. The honest answer is… It's gonna be challenging, but even in this. You can find your voice and place in making a difference and being the hero your peers and other young black males need. How can you take action? I'm glad you asked:

- ❖ **Talk about it** - Talk to a friend or trusted adult.
- ❖ **Unplug** - Be Careful what you allow yourself to watch and listen to.
- ❖ **Find a Mentor** - There are resources and organizations around the country waiting for you to sign up. Here are a few:
  - ➢ 100 Black Men of America
  - ➢ OK Program
  - ➢ Mentoring Kings

If you feel like giving up. GET HELP! CALL 1 800 273-8255

National Suicide Prevention line

Chapter 7

Envy is a criminal.

Envy is real. I have seen folks do things in their 20s that I am confident I could have done but didn't dare to go through with. The people I see advancing are doing great things, don't get me wrong, but I need to deal with that internal thing within me. It's not to the point where I hate the individual. It becomes a frustration within me that says if I could get my stuff together, I could be there also.

But you gotta remember...Everyone's journey is different.

Point 1: You should be rare. Being great is lonely at times. Do you ever wonder why you only have a few friends? Do you look and see everyone around you "in the crew." I've learned to become comfortable in the lonely. Sometimes it's frustrating not having anyone to call and check on you. It's as if no one cares. But let me tell you something, God has a plan for you that you were destined for. Looking at most of our pioneers, you will find they have few friends. You won't see group photos. Once you learn to embrace your place, you realize more about yourself. You recognize your greatness. I'm not saying to ignore folks or anything; I'm saying that don't be discouraged by being lonely. Be encouraged by the fact that people will look to you for guidance. Don't let your identity be wrapped up in the people you follow.

Use envy as motivation. I know there is frustration when you see someone doing what you know you are called to do. There is no hate towards that person, but you may be frustrated that you want to be in that position. It varies in the amount of time it will take to get over. Your most important task at this point in the journey is recognizing where you are in the journey itself. How you get to where you want to be should be written on paper. As you go through, you can look at your map and say, "This is where I'm at." A common mistake is we look at others folks' maps and confuse theirs with ours. The destination may be the same, but I promise how you get there will be different.

Envy isn't healthy at all but listen to this. What would it take for "YOU" to be envied? You have to wonder how much you want it. Envy is nothing but a distraction that keeps you from your mission. Your eyes should be focused on your community. Everyone is waiting on you to start. Someone is waiting for you to get them out of the living hell that they are going through. Your family is waiting for you to take charge and deliver the family out of their circumstances. I know. It's a lot of weight. Some may say that you don't deserve this. You may say that you wish you had mentors to help. But guess what? You were built for this. God used everything that you've been through.

Story Time:

I had been reading God's Word every day. I had heard Him speaking to me as if He was right next to me at the kitchen table. Our pastor had brought a guest speaker in, and he was going to preach. Internally I thought, Why didn't he ask me to preach?" Does he not see me? Does he not know the difference between me? As he was speaking, I zoned out and imagined myself on the same stage at that exact time. Everything he was saying, I knew. The revelation that he got, I felt like I received as well. The frustration at that point wasn't about the guest speaker or my pastor. It became aggravating because I wanted to be there, but it wasn't my time yet.

Your Turn

Who do you envy (look up to), and why?

____

____

____

____

How will you use your envy to fuel your passions?

____

____

____

____

What step can you take today to start moving in the right direction?

____

____

____

____

Chapter 8

You are someone's Hero

God has made and prepared me to be an original, not a duplicate. I have this incredible ability to encourage others and be transparent about my feelings. Depending on who you hang around, some may need help handling your authentic version. Don't let that stop you.

Someone needs the authentic version to get out of the hell they are going through. Someone needs to know they are not the only ones going through this. You will realize that once you start doing you and walking in your purpose - you will automatically start to feel more confident. Your walk will be different. You will begin to talk differently. You will become the authentic version of yourself.

Living a transparent life is sometimes the best example for people. Have you ever heard people say, 'I'm just keeping it real"? However, in most instances, they are tearing people down and not lifting them up. Can we start having folks that are keeping it real in a way that they are motivating folks to be better versions of themselves?

When someone tells you how you have changed their life, it's incredible! Imagine waking up and saying, I am going to show people the real me today, only to go in front of friends and others as the person you think they want. People will only receive true healing when you unmask the person that you were and begin to speak who you really are. Being you can come with some risks.

You are asking yourself if people would accept the real you. They will see my real faults and shortcomings. They may not like that. I am here to tell you that those people may not be your audience. You have to understand that you are a brand now. You can never fail to be the real you. Even on your worst day, you can be authentic and not worry about "making a mistake."

You realize the things that you've been through made you who you are. Think right now of all the hard times that you have gone through. Think about the unfair things you didn't have any control over. Recognize that some of it was out of your control. We can't separate ourselves from our decisions, but we can choose this day to use all of that to make a difference, not just in our lives but in the folks' lives around us.

Story Time: Lawanda and I were facilitating our weekly marriage group. During the middle of class, one of the fellas raised his hand. I acknowledged him and said what you got, bro. He said what I am about to tell you is one of the hardest things I have ever been through. Still, because you have been so transparent, I have the confidence to bring this up in front of the entire group (Our class consisted of about 20 couples). He began to say, "I haven't had a relationship with my daughter because of how myself and her mother split up. However, after being in this group, I have the courage to make things right." While he said this, I cried because of the weight of responsibility, knowing that my honesty gives people hope. After he was done, all 40 or so of us embraced him, prayed with him, and told him that we would have his back.

Let me Help You, Help You…

❖ Do a self-check on who you really are.

Describe the real authentic you.

____

____

____

____

Write about some of the hard things that you have been through. Talk about how you will use them to be a good influence on your peers and younger siblings.

____

____

____

____

Chapter 9

Don't be afraid to connect.

Word on the streets is that it's easier to do things on your own. When you look at pioneers, you may only see one person, but you may not see the many people that add to the bigger picture.

Opportunity knocks, and when it does, answer the door.

There have been opportunities. You have gotten in the right circles. You have even been to a couple of group meetings but have yet to start engaging. Why not? What are you scared of? You may have seen other people's relationships end badly because of bad business deals or miscommunication. However, please take advantage of the opportunity to grow because you didn't allow yourself to explore it first. Now I'm not telling you to go out and pour your feelings or dreams out to everyone (that would be a wrong move), but at least consider every opportunity with a list of requirements that you set to determine how you want to proceed with the relationship. The list could look something like this: What is their track record (criminal, business, how they treat family, etc.).

Don't be selfish. There is someone that needs you. Even if it is someone younger, your age, or maybe even older. I have been around young people that have inspired me to be a better version of myself. You have to be willing to give something you didn't even think you had (love, respect, conversation, etc.). As you navigate this book, take the time to provide what you have learned to someone who may need it.

Name a few people that have reached out to you to join their circle? What did that conversation look like?

____

____

____

____

Ask three people to describe you using one word. How did it make you feel?

____

____

____

____

Chapter 10

Who's on your team?

Who is in your starting lineup? In finding out who you are, you have to identify the people in your life that will; push you in the right direction if you stumble, stop, or misdirect. My closest friends are the ones who bring me the most value.

Choose wisely. All the people in your life aren't_meant to coach you. Know the difference! Some people are there to see you walk out what you said you would do. Some people are there to witness your journey. It would help if you had those too. Unfortunately, you may not know how to identify who is who, but you should think carefully about who you choose to direct you where you are going.

Your time starts now. Identify where you are in your journey, pray, and acknowledge where you are now. Then talk with the people in your life. Start normal conversations.

- Do you know anyone interested in seeing you reach your goals? If not, your circle needs to change.
- Do you have someone that asks you how you are feeling? If not, you need one.
- Do you have anyone that says how I can help you get to where you're going? If not, you need one.

To be clear, if you don't have these folks in your life but have friends, assign them jobs. Most times, friends only know how they can help you if you tell them.

Time to activate. Once you get these people in place, you begin to release who you really are. You recognize your strengths and what you can offer to your community. You can offer this to the many people who look up to you. I encourage you to be Strong. Be courageous. Be bold.

Let me Help You, Help You…

❖ Your community awaits.

How are you choosing to be a part of your team?

____

____

____

____

How are you actively helping your community and the people around you?

____

____

____

____

Who keeps you accountable? Name three people.

____

____

____

____

How has this book changed the way you see yourself?